Staff Retention
in a week

SUE BROWELL

Hodder & Stoughton
BRB
A MEMBER OF THE HODDER HEADLINE GROUP

As the champion of management, the
Chartered Management Institute shapes and
supports the managers of tomorrow. By sharing
intelligent insights and setting standards in
management development, the Institute helps
to deliver results in a dynamic world.

chartered

management

institute

inspiring leaders

For more information call 01536 204222 or visit www.managers.org.uk

Orders: please contact Bookpoint Ltd, 130 Milton Park, Abingdon, Oxon
OX14 4TD. Telephone: (44) 01235 827720. Fax: (44) 01235 400454. Lines are open
from 9.00–6.00, Monday to Saturday, with a 24 hour message answering service.
Email address: orders@bookpoint.co.uk

British Library Cataloguing in Publication Data
A catalogue record for this title is available from The British Library

ISBN 0 340 849738

First published   2001
Impression number   10 9 8 7 6 5 4 3 2 1
Year   2007 2006 2005 2004 2003

Cover image: Stone/Getty Images

Typeset by SX Composing DTP, Rayleigh, Essex.
Printed in Great Britain for Hodder & Stoughton Educational, a division of
Hodder Headline Plc, 338 Euston Road, London NW1 3BH.

■■■■ C O N T E N T S ■■■■

Staff retention is one of the most important issues within organisations and can influence its success. If the best staff are not retained then organisations may not retain key clients and customers. Keeping valuable staff can be a source of competitive advantage. Their knowledge, expertise and skills can contribute to the long-term success of an organisation. You need to attract good people, use them effectively and reward them so you keep the staff you want. You also need to accept that some staff will leave and this is not always negative. The process is therefore attract, recruit, induct, develop, reward, retain and separate. It costs money when you lose staff, costs money to keep them but failing to deal with staff retention can potentially affect financial performance and reduce an organisation's profits. Staff retention is not a simple issue but if you want to keep your best staff then you need to take action.

This book is intended for managers, team leaders and human resource specialists who need to understand their role in staff retention and the action they need to take. If they are to be successful, they need to understand the following that we shall look at during this week:

- What staff retention is and why it is important to organisations
- How to identify whether you have a problem with staff retention
- How to assess and measure staff retention
- The reasons why some staff leave and others stay
- How to keep them now and in the future
- The benefits and disadvantages of staff retention
- The costs of staff retention
- The people who need to be involved.

Staff retention – what it is all about

Today, we will examine:

- What is staff retention?
- When does staff retention begin?
- Changing nature of organisations
- Changing nature of work

What is staff retention?

In simple terms, staff retention means keeping those members of staff that one wants to keep and not losing them from the organisation, for whatever reason, but especially to competitors. Organisations need to have the right people with the right skills and abilities in the right place at the right time. This relies on planning, effective recruitment, selection, training, development, retaining those you want to keep and recognising the time for separation. Thinking about the following questions is a useful starting point:

- What is the value of good staff?
- How do you define good or key members of staff – knowledge, expertise, high performance, commitment, loyalty, creativity, high educational qualifications, talent, technical competence?
- What is special about your organisation and why should people come and work in it?
- What makes your organisation an attractive place to work in and how do you attract people?

The survival and success of organisations in the next few

years will mostly depend upon their staff. People can and do make a difference to organisations and are often their most valuable assets. Talented staff can improve organisation performance. Inter-related and integrative policies, a focus on performance, motivation, training and development are all linked to effective management of people and to competitive advantage. It is important that an organisation understands:

- The environment in which it exists
- The pressures it faces
- What it has to do to change and adapt
- The contribution of its staff to improvement and innovation
- Cost effectiveness in an increasingly competitive world.

Good members of staff
Good staff are often referred to as key or prized staff because they are so important to the success of an organisation who place significant emphasis on their retention. Certain positions within an organisation, for example strategic or technical, are

vital to its success, and a vacancy in one of these positions could cause immediate problems for the organisation. The staff in these positions are extremely important because of their skills, knowledge and expertise. They are seen as a source of competitive advantage, crucial to high-performing organisations. The ability to retain these talented, key members of staff is one of the most important issues facing all organisations around the world. For some organisations, retaining such staff is becoming more and more difficult. You need to look at the skills and abilities of your own staff:

- Do they have what the organisation wants and needs? If the answer is yes, then you probably need to retain them
- Who are your most valuable and vulnerable employees who might be attractive to head-hunters and competitors?

When does staff retention begin?

Staff retention begins long before recruitment. You might think that this is strange and retention will only begin once you have staff working within the organisation. However, you need to consider whether the organisation has a good reputation and is somewhere that people want to work. Organisations need to focus on employer brand to both attract and retain staff and this requires more than websites and glossy brochures. For organisations to be recognised as an employer of choice, a good reputation must exist in all parts of the organisation. If it is not a good place to work and you have difficulty keeping staff then you will probably not attract good people. The details that you put in job advertisements, how enquiries are handled and the actual recruitment and selection process all say something about the organisation. If you are not accurate and honest then any new members of staff may leave quickly.

Changing nature of organisations

In the past twenty years or so, downsizing, cost reduction, restructuring, outsourcing, mergers and acquisitions and organisational changes have eroded staff loyalty. A lack of security and a view that career development is a personal responsibility has resulted in individuals believing their only choice for career progression is to change employers.

Organisations are changing and there is a need to understand both what is happening inside the organisation and in the external environment. The external factors that affect your organisation are political, economic, social, technological, legal and environmental. These are important when examining skills shortages, demographic issues, competitors and the government, and can have a major influence on staff retention. You need to understand how these factors can cause problems. You also need to understand what is happening inside the organisation in terms of structure, size, culture, management style etc. These are some of the issues you need to consider:

- Organisations – structure and size
- Economic situation
- Labour market and composition of workforce
- Skills and skills shortages
- Demographic issues
- Regional variations
- Knowledge management

Organisations – structure and size
Many organisations have reduced in size, restructured, removed levels of management and reduced the numbers of staff. These have implications for staff retention.

- How do you keep the staff you want?
- How do you continue to motivate remaining staff when many of their friends and colleagues have gone?
- Remaining staff may be disillusioned and demotivated, with reduced commitment and loyalty
- Key skills, qualities and knowledge are in demand and, with fewer staff, employers need to attract and keep their most valuable staff
- The future is much more about development, quality of life, benefits and rewards
- Organisations cannot keep paying more and more simply to attract and retain key staff.

There are differences between small and large organisations, type and sector and these are important regarding the approaches taken. Mergers and acquisitions have caused some changes often creating large organisations, but there are usually more people than jobs, resulting in casualties. In addition, some staff may not like the changes and leave. This then becomes a staff retention issue.

Economic situation
Economic situations affect staff turnover and retention. Low unemployment means people have greater choice over where they work therefore attracting and retaining good staff is a number one issue. If there are economic difficulties or a recession with high unemployment, staff will often stay with an employer even though they are unhappy and potentially unproductive. When the economic situation improves, they may then leave. If the economy is strong with lots of job opportunities, some staff may be tempted to leave, adding to staff retention problems.

Labour market and composition of workforce
The labour market comprises those able to work, whether in employment or looking for employment and is the place where employers go when they need new staff. You need to consider labour and skills shortages, demographic issues, the proportion of people in and out of work, regional issues, age profiles, gender balance, availability of part-time and temporary employees, competition and geographical location of the organisation. These issues are important and will determine whether the staff you want are available and can also help to explain why some of your staff may be leaving. In many countries, the labour market is changing. In some, there are more women in the workforce, an ageing population, high

unemployment and individuals prepared to accept part-time work. However, many vacancies are proving difficult to fill even in areas of high unemployment because potential staff do not have the skills required. Employers need to be aware of changes in labour markets and take action, consider what potential new staff want, in times of increased competition, as many may not accept jobs because they do not like the hours and conditions. When there are difficulties, employers can do a number of things. They can:

- Compete more aggressively regarding recruitment initiatives, pay, organisation image etc
- Provide more training, access to training or retraining
- Improve the utilisation of existing staff and/or look at reducing wastage
- Look at the composition of the workforce – a diverse workforce can make it easier to attract and retain staff
- Look at the recruitment and retention of all staff, particularly women and older staff.

Skills and skills shortages
An organisation whose staff have the right skills potentially has competitive advantage. Skills shortages are caused by changes in:

- The nature of work
- Technology
- The skills required by organisations
- Demography
- The composition of workforce.

Employers need to be aware of global shortages of talented and qualified staff and how this affects them. There is evidence of skills shortages in many countries and sectors, including both new and traditional skills. You must determine whether there is a lack of labour or a lack of knowledge and expertise. In some organisations, a lack of investment in apprenticeships, initial training courses, education, training and development together with a poor image of some skilled jobs has resulted in skills shortages and people not entering certain sectors. Multi-skilling provides generalist skills and can result in subcontracting, use of overtime and temporary members of staff. Retention is important because of the gap between the demand for and the supply of skilled staff. If there are skills shortages, the following questions should be asked, to find out what you can do as an employer:

- Are you affected by a shortage of school leavers?
- Can you establish relationships with schools and colleges?
- Can you train existing staff so they have the skills where there are shortages?
- How many graduates are there available?
- Do they have the skills you require?

If skills shortages exist, consider under represented groups such as women, over 55s, Internet generation and global workforce. Employers need to be more creative in dealing with shortages.

Demographic issues
Employers need to understand demographic issues and how they affect the organisation. Organisations need to anticipate and react to the demographic changes that countries experience, to help them move from traditional to more modern sources of labour and working methods. The type of population a country has is important.

- Young population – many people under age of 20, high birth and mortality rates; few adults and many unemployed young people
- Adult population – decreasing birth and mortality rates; high proportion of adults, large labour markets
- Elderly population – increase in number of people over 60, few children; decrease in available workforce
- Declining population – very low birth rate, large proportion of elderly people eventually resulting in overall decline of population; insufficient workforce.

Low birth rates can result in few young people entering labour markets. Organisations need to consider adopting family friendly policies, part-time working, not being ageist, as well as ensuring effective human resource and succession planning. Demographic changes require organisations to critically examine the composition of workforces as follows as these issues can affect staff retention:

- Age profile
- Number of graduates
- Number of women and men
- Number of school leavers
- Cultural and ethnic mix.

Regional variations
The need to focus on staff retention can vary between regions as well as between countries. In certain parts of any country there may be shortages of particular skills with employers competing for the same staff. However, there may also be areas of high unemployment where retention is not an issue.

Knowledge management
This is concerned with retaining and sharing knowledge and
expertise. Knowledge-based competition is increasing and
staff retention is even more important when staff have specific
knowledge, expertise and intellectual capital. What value do
you place on knowledge and can you afford to lose it?

Changing nature of work

Organisations continue to change as does the nature of work.
Additionally, the expectations of existing and prospective
staff are changing. It is easier to change jobs and also to work
from home. Nevertheless, employers still need people, but
how do we manage staff effectively to increase commitment
and performance? What practical policies can we put in place
to ensure staff commitment and retention, especially when
long-term employment cannot be guaranteed? An
organisation's culture and values are important, together
with work ethics, loyalty and how managers treat their

employees. Many organisations refer to their staff as *human capital* because of the knowledge and experience they bring to the organisation/workplace. People are seen to make a difference to the success of an organisation and add value. It is important to understand how the nature of work differs from that of our parents and grandparents, as well as how it has changed over the past few years. The following have implications for staff retention:

- Flexible working and flexibility
- Working practices
- Working hours
- Technology
- Contracts
- Emotional intelligence

Flexible working and flexibility
Flexibility can be considered in a number of different ways:

- Functional or task flexibility – staff able to perform different tasks and use a variety of skills
- Numerical flexibility – staff numbers, use of short-term contracts, part-time hours, subcontracting etc
- Temporal flexibility – variation in working hours and the use of flexible hours
- Wage or financial flexibility – individualised pay and reward systems based on performance. Move away from standardised pay structures.

If employers use numerical flexibility, they must carefully consider the staff they wish to retain as key staff before subcontracting or adopting flexible working, such as part-time, home-working or job-sharing. Temporary staff can add to staff turnover and decrease an organisation's effectiveness and profitability. Organisations need some permanent staff but can use a variety of other staff and agencies on a non-permanent basis.

Many organisations are introducing more flexible working practices and changes including the following:

- Variations in the composition of the workforce
- More part-time and flexible staff
- Increased responsibility for staff – requiring training and development, increased awareness of motivation, performance management
- Fewer staff but more skilled
- Different working hours and place of work
- Flexible benefits and rewards.

Working practices
There are significant variations in working practices often requiring individual flexibility and responsibility, as well as team-working. Flatter organisations with few hierarchies can give staff increased responsibility and autonomy and can often improve staff retention and communication. However, they also lack vertical promotion opportunities and can contribute towards some staff leaving.

Working hours
In some organisations and in some countries, working excessively long hours is a problem. The long hours culture can be a result of lack of staff, too much work or expectations of managers and colleagues. Working long hours can break the law and be demotivating leading to increased absence, stress and staff turnover. It can be harmful to individuals and does not

necessarily benefit the organisation in terms of productivity and can create a poor image. Some organisations have introduced incentives for staff to work smarter and shorter hours.

Technology
Technology, such as computers, e-mail and the Internet, are changing both how people work and where they work. Technology has been responsible for changing specific jobs, such as secretaries, and reducing the amount of paperwork and administrative duties associated with many other jobs. The use of e-mail has also helped to improve communication between staff regardless of where they may be working. Technology has also enabled some people to work while travelling, or to work from home. This can have benefits for staff and employers and improve staff retention.

Traditional Working	Flexible Working
Full-time	Part-time, job-sharing
Based at employer's premises	Can be home-based or mixture of home- and employer-based
Regular 9–5 weekday hours	Various/flexible hours
Part-time staff viewed as being less committed, more difficult to retain and not as valuable as full-time staff	Part-time staff seen as equal partners
Different rights and benefits for full-time and part-time staff	Equal (or equivalent) rights for full-time and part-time staff

Contracts
Traditional employment relationships were based on job security, trust and loyalty but these attitudes have been eroded by downsizing and other changes and a job for life rarely exists. New contracts are more individually based rather than

collectively negotiated and acknowledge the different values and needs of staff. The focus is more on partnership, mutual benefits and an acceptance that staff will move through the organisation and then leave. The relationship between organisation, work and individual member of staff forms the psychological contract. These contracts need to acknowledge different expectations concerning behaviour, attitudes, feelings, treatment and the relationship between employer and employee.

Emotional intelligence
This concept is concerned with recognising our own and others' feelings and the effective management of emotions and relationships. Those managers with low emotional intelligence may not recognise the value of their staff and try to control them, while those with high emotional intelligence recognise that staff have their own needs and tend to be able to relate to them more easily and be more tolerant. They are more willing to delegate, are open, give feedback and are more able to retain staff.

Summary

Today we learnt what staff retention is. We know that:

- Staff retention is about keeping those members of staff that one wants to keep
- Good staff are important to the success of an organisation
- Organisations are changing and are affected by many different factors
- The nature of work is also changing with an increase in flexible working and changes in working practices.

How do you know you have got a problem?

Today, we will examine:

- Assessments and measurements
- Staff turnover rates
- Stability and retention rates
- Other assessments and measurements

Organisations must first recognise that they have a problem, understand its causes and then take action. You need to **PAUSE**:

Problem identification
Analysis
Understand the reasons
Solutions/recommendations
Evaluate and review success of solutions/
  recommendations

Examining the past and the present may provide clues as to how to deal with the future. You need to understand the causes of staff turnover in order to implement solutions and improve staff retention. Consider the following before you begin:

- Why do some people not want to work for your organisation?
- Why do some people reject/not accept job offers?
- What attracts some people to join your organisation as new members of staff?
- Why do some people continue to stay in the organisation?
- How can you find out why staff are leaving?
- How can you prevent staff leaving or slow down the rate?

- What is causing staff turnover?
- Ask employees what is important to them.

Assessments and measurements

You need to collect information from people who want to
leave or have left, as well as from those who stay, so you
understand their reasons and what you can do to keep staff.
Staff turnover can be predicted. Generally if staff are asked if
they intend to stay with the organisation and answer no, then
they will leave. Potential, current and former staff all need to
be spoken to so you get an accurate picture.

Employers need to know what data to collect and analyse and
have efficient information systems to assist in recording data and
analysis. The data should be objective and specific to enable
accurate diagnosis and to ensure effective and realistic solutions
and strategies are put in place. This includes identifying the
factors that have the greatest chance of improving commitment
and retention. There are lots of different assessments and
measurements that can be used to measure staff turnover,
morale, staff retention and other issues. These include:

- Surveys and discussion groups
- Absenteeism
- Performance and appraisals
- Career development
- Exit interviews/questionnaires
- Talent audit
- Benchmarking
- Risk analysis

Surveys and discussion groups
Attitude or opinion surveys examine the attitudes and perceptions of staff towards their job and the organisation/employer. These are often used when organisations begin to encounter problems or difficulties and they need to understand why, as they can identify critical factors. Some employers also conduct surveys regularly to gather positive and negative feedback from their staff. They provide up-to-date data on how staff are feeling, they demonstrate management interest and they provide opportunities for improvement and future development. Attitude surveys include one-to-one interviews, discussion groups or questionnaires and can be general or very specific. Surveys are used to gain information about:

- Management and leadership
- Communication, values, mission, strategy and vision
- Organisational structures, climate and culture
- Policies, procedures and administration
- Planning, including target-setting and appraisal
- Motivation and commitment of staff, including morale
- Relationships and interactions with others
- Staff involvement and recognition

- Decision-making and empowerment
- Learning, training and development
- Staff thinking of leaving.

All of the above are important in relation to staff retention. However, attitude surveys need careful planning if they are to be successful. First of all, the purpose and content of the survey should be clear, both to management and staff who will be surveyed. Then, you should consider the use of questionnaires versus face-to-face contact. Questionnaires are useful when staff numbers are large, but interviews and group discussions will generate different information. A combination of both approaches is possible and useful. When using a questionnaire, you should spend time writing, designing and piloting it, to avoid ambiguities. You should also:

- Keep questionnaires short and confidential
- Use rating scales, with lots of tick boxes; open-ended questions are more difficult to compare
- Consider time-scales and when surveys are conducted; at busy times, information may be limited
- Consider who to survey – everyone or a sample?

Discussion groups usually comprise a facilitator and approximately eight staff. Facilitators ask questions such as:

- Why do you stay?
- Why would you leave?
- Why do people leave?
- Why do people join?
- Why do they not join?
- How can the organisation recruit?
- How can the organisation retain its employees?

Once the surveys are completed, the information must be analysed, which can be done by computers. Then, the results should be shared with staff. This can be by formal presentation, e-mail, to small groups, in a report. Make sure that something happens as a result of the survey, as action demonstrates commitment by managers. It may result in a change to practices and policies. Surveys should be conducted at regular intervals to allow for comparisons over time. They should be part of the organisation's communication process, and one that reflects its culture.

If surveys are completed by existing staff, potential leavers and those who have already left, the information can be compared. This helps identify and explain the causes of staff turnover and doing something about it can help improve staff retention.

Absenteeism
Staff retention can be linked to absence. Staff who are frequently absent may be considering leaving and may be attending job interviews. It is important to monitor absence figures, weekly, monthly and annually, conduct return-to-

work interviews, and try to determine the causes of the absence. Consider incentives for good attendance and penalties for frequent and unacceptable absence.

Performance and appraisals

Information about performance and productivity can highlight issues concerning staff morale. Team, group and organisation performance can be indicators of job satisfaction. Appraisals provide information about individual performance, attitudes and perceptions. They give staff the opportunity to sit down with their immediate line manager and discuss issues such as motivation, career development, communication, recognition, target-setting, learning, training and education. Job satisfaction, conditions, relationships with others, pay and benefits can also be discussed.

Career development

Career development interviews and/or questionnaires are helpful to line managers, human resource specialists and the organisation in determining what staff want and what their career aspirations are. They can assist in predicting who is likely to stay or leave because if staff have specific desires that the organisation cannot fulfil, then they may leave. Career development questionnaires and interviews usually contain the following questions:

- Job title/position, sector
- What other roles have you had?
- How many years have you been working in this sector?
- What other sectors have you worked in?
- Is current job full-time, part-time, fixed-term, other?
- When did you move to your current job?

- When do you intend to leave your current employer?
- How many times have you changed jobs during your working life, including internal promotion?
- How many of the job changes have been for promotion?
- What factors influenced your last move, e.g. redundancy, promotion, restructuring, relationship with colleagues and management, change of career, work/life balance, more challenging job, pay and reward, travel/location of organisation, stress/health issues, other?
- How satisfied are you with your career to date and what factors will influence your next move?
- Are you satisfied with your current position and the opportunities with your current employer?
- How satisfied are you with work life balance?
- What factors are important to you in a job – working hours, salary and benefits, job security, promotion, interesting and challenging work, ability to make decisions, the people, the organisation?
- Does your organisation support the management of your career and what help would you like?
- When did you last update your CV, undergo an interview or an assessment centre?

Not all questions will be asked by all organisations at all times. However, if an organisation is genuinely concerned about its staff, questionnaires will often be issued for them to return anonymously, as part of regular surveys of staff attitudes. They may also form the basis of discussions between line managers and their staff.

Exit interviews/questionnaires
These provide data as to why people leave and can identify some problems and causes. They need to be undertaken

properly or not at all, and they do take time. Information from both interviews and questionnaires should observe confidentiality. Exit interviews should be conducted by an independent person – human resource specialist, someone from another department or a consultant experienced in interviewing – not by the immediate line manager. Interviews can help the person who is leaving say things they might not otherwise have said. It can help if they are scheduled away from the normal workplace and ideally should take place at the time someone resigns or just before they leave. At end of interview (if they cannot be persuaded to stay), wish staff good luck, thank them for their services and state you hope/would like to work with them again in the future – if you want to keep them.

Questionnaires are similar to exit interview forms and can be used when interviews are impossible or inappropriate. They allow individuals to respond in their own way and own time, can be anonymous and are therefore potentially more revealing. Questionnaires should be issued a few weeks after the person has left. Interviews/questionnaires can determine some problems and reasons for leaving and can also provide information about competitors. However, they should not be used in isolation as exit interviews and questionnaires are not totally reliable. Leavers will not always be honest, or tell you everything and staff will give limited information if they:

- Want to return to the organisation at a later date
- Are concerned that references will be affected
- Are too polite
- Do not care enough about the company
- Are leaving for reasons that they feel are too sensitive to discuss openly (bullying, harassment).

Exit Interview Form/Questionnaire

Name .... Current position .... Department/location ....

Hours of work .... Pay (per week/year) .... Manager ....

Age .... Gender .... Ethnic group ....

Start date .... Leaving date ....

Working in the organisation

1. Why did you want to work in this organisation?
2. What have been the best and worst aspects?
3. What would you like to change and why?
4. What if anything would encourage you to stay?

Reasons for leaving

Please indicate your main reason(s) for leaving:

Personal betterment/promotion	☐	Inadequate induction	☐
Job uninteresting/boring/ insufficient challenge	☐	Dissatisfaction with conditions/ work environment	☐
Lack of training and development	☐	Dissatisfaction with hours	☐
Dissatisfaction with pay	☐	Dissatisfaction with benefits	☐
Travelling difficulties	☐	Dissatisfaction with colleagues	☐
Change in personal circumstances	☐	Workload/stress	☐
Dissatisfaction with team leader/manager	☐	Lack of promotion opportunities and career development	☐
Family responsibilities	☐	Other (please specify)	☐

Have you obtained another job?

If yes

Name of employer .... Location .... Job title ....

Pay .... Hours .... Other benefits ....

If no

Further study	☐	Self-employment	☐
Not working	☐	Other (please specify)	☐

To be completed by organisation representative. Interviewer's name/position

....

Would you re-employ this employee .... Date of interview ....

Compare information from leavers with surveys and those still working for the organisation. Use this to anticipate problems and take action. Remember that collecting data is useful but it must be analysed to establish trends. Compare part-timers and full-timers, age, gender, length of service etc.

Sometimes it is useful to contact former staff who have left in the past 6-18 months and who the organisation would have liked to keep. Such contacts by telephone interview or questionnaire are often conducted by an independent person to ensure confidentiality. They aim to identify key causes of staff turnover using a variety of data and recommend actions to increase and improve staff retention.

Talent audit
Auditing your workforce to ensure you know what talent you have is important to career development and staff retention. If you have a number of talented staff can you satisfy their aspirations and needs? If not, they may leave. If you have insufficient talented staff what are the implications for the success of the organisation?

Benchmarking

Where staff turnover and retention difficulties exist, benchmarking is often considered, although many organisations undertake benchmarking regularly and not just when there are problems. Benchmarking is a process of measuring and critically examining processes, practices, systems, performance and numbers against other internal departments, business units and/or other organisations. A benchmark is a reference point or standard against which measurements can be made. So who do you benchmark against and how?

- Benchmark against the best organisations, then the best within your industry/sector and finally internal benchmarking
- Use industry surveys, customer/supplier interviews, networking within professional bodies and one-to-one interviews
- Compare staff turnover and retention, absenteeism, pay and rewards. Be careful – data itself may not provide the information you need. Critically examine and get behind the practices of those you are benchmaking against
- Benchmarking and collecting information allows you to learn from the experience and knowledge of others in order to improve
- You must fully understand how your organisation works, its problems and practices before benchmarking against others and then applying the knowledge and information
- Benchmarking requires detailed and effective preparation
- The wrong benchmark, lack of preparation or no follow-up action will result in poor outcomes or lack of success.

Risk analysis

Employing and keeping staff can be a risky business. Investing in staff that you then lose costs time and wastes resources. You

need to consider who is more or less likely to leave. It is possible
to determine the risk by identifying and analysing issues. Risk
analysis examines the chances, consequences and impact on the
organisation of someone leaving. Where the impact of someone
leaving is low, then the problem is not significant, although can
still cost money and have a negative effect on staff morale.
However, when the impact of staff leaving is high then this
needs to be considered more seriously and organisations need to
focus on staff retention even if the chance of them leaving is low.
It becomes even more important when the chances of them
leaving is high. Employers should be aware that staff leaving
affects remaining staff and may increase staff turnover and costs.

- What would happen if a particular member of staff left
  your organisation?
- What are the chances of this happening – high/medium/low?
- Is there a link between qualifications, experience, length of
  service and other issues and the chance of them leaving?
- Who would you be sorry to lose, what would be the cost
  and how serious would the loss be?
- How easy would it be for you to replace the person?
- What would be the effects on production/customers if the
  person joined your competitors?

Several factors influence who is more or less likely to leave
an organisation. These include:

- Higher education qualifications
- Unhappy with life in general
- The balance between home and work is wrong
- Poor psychological contract
- Demonstrates low commitment

- High level of involvement at home and low level of involvement at work
- Wants greater direct participation.

Have you considered staff retention in relation to strategic planning and risk management in terms of increased costs of turnover and potential loss of competitive advantage?

Staff turnover rates

Staff turnover is closely related to retention and can highlight problem areas. Turnover refers to starters and leavers in an organisation, including voluntary and involuntary leavers. For staff retention, we really need to focus on voluntary leavers. Turnover, and the impact it has on an organisation, can be measured and analysed in a number of different ways.

Number of staff leaving in a given period
(e.g. monthly, quarterly, annually)   x 100
Average number employed during the same period

(The average number employed in the same period can be calculated by adding together the number of employees in post at the beginning and at the end of the period and dividing by two)

Example
    Number leaving   12
    Average number employed   60
    Staff turnover $\frac{12}{60}$ x 100   = 20%

Such figures do not give an accurate view of staff leaving. The figures include anyone dismissed, come to the end of their contract, retired or made redundant. The percentage rate alone is not enough to understand the problem because all leavers are included. It provides some information but hides the real causes. A lower overall figure one year compared to the previous year may actually include an increase in voluntary turnover if involuntary turnover has reduced. Wherever possible try to use the data for those people who are leaving voluntarily as this group is the most important when considering retention and the one that employers have least control over. Ideally you should examine data by:

- Job role/occupation or grade
- Number of working hours (full- or part-time)
- Department, Business Unit and geographical location
- Length of service
- Age and gender
- Education, qualifications, graduates.

Sometimes travel to work, distance, time of year and dependants may also be significant. Examining specific data helps to explain problems and determine why people leave. High turnover may not be a universal problem but may be restricted to a job, section or length of service. You need to examine trends and look carefully at the information you have. Staff turnover should be analysed regularly – weekly, monthly and annually if necessary – so you can begin to establish trends.

You should ask yourself:

- What do you consider is a normal staff turnover rate for your organisation?
- Has the rate increased, decreased or stayed the same in the past year?
- Do you think staff turnover is too high, unusually low or neither in your organisation?

Examining staff turnover together with information from exit interviews and questionnaires can be useful but is not simple. Figures can be misleading so you should carefully examine all available data and information and avoid jumping to conclusions. Compare with other employers as well as with your own annual rates. Staff turnover involves costs for the organisation and we shall look at these in Friday.

Stability and retention rates

Examining stability rates takes the opposite view to staff turnover and focuses on staff that are retained and not on the ones that have left. Stability and retention rates can be calculated for the organisation as a whole or for particular groups or departments. Rates provide an indication of how many staff remain in an organisation as a percentage of those leaving/joining. The rates are determined by the numbers of staff at a particular time divided by the number of staff employed at the start of that time period expressed as a percentage.

$$\frac{\text{Number with minimum one year's service}}{\text{Total number employed a year ago}} \times 100$$

In the earlier staff turnover example, 12 leavers could have done 12 different jobs or they could all have done the same job but only stayed four weeks. Therefore, there may be evidence of staff turnover but the workforce is mainly stable.

Number with one year's service	55		
Employed a year ago	60		
Stability rate	$\frac{55}{60}$	× 100	= 91.7%

55 staff have been employed for more than one year (and may have significant length of service) and hence the stability rate is 91.7%.

Figures only tell part of the story and there should be further analysis, interpretation and consideration of the implications. Typically, we would expect to find the following relationships between turnover and stability rates.

Turnover rate	Stability rate	Implication
High	Low	High turnover in most jobs
High	High	High turnover in a small number of jobs
Low	High	Stable workforce
Low	Low	Possible problem with figures – recount

Other assessments and measurements

These include things like involvement in teams, volunteers, response rates to surveys, accidents, grievances, recruitment trends and strikes. These all tell you something about how people are within the organisation and help clarify what staff want and how they are in comparison to what managers, team leaders and others believe. Specific audits or assessments of stress also provide important information about how people feel. Jobs where there is pressure and the potential for stress should be identified. Information from staff turnover, working hours, absenteeism, attitude surveys, accidents and customer satisfaction surveys will also provide important details when considering stress. Staff records can be useful in terms of age profile, length of service, distance travelling to work and can be used to analyse trends and understand why certain staff leave, such as temporary staff. It is also useful to assess the use of benefits by level, person and group. The assessment and measurement of costs are dealt with in Friday. Assessing human resource policies and procedures is also important. Consider the following:

- Do recruitment and selection policies fit and match what the organisation wants?
- Are the right selection methods used?
- What about performance management and reward?
- Does it match local market?
- Does it motivate staff?
- Is training and development evaluated?
- Does it achieve the objectives set out?
- Does it contribute to individual and organisational improvement?

Analysing human resources data contributes to effective human resource planning. Once you've analysed, assessed and measured, then you need to take action and do something about the problem.

Summary

Today we have learnt about assessing and measuring staff turnover and retention:

- Information from assessments and measurements should be analysed so you begin to understand the problem and its causes
- Data should be collected from current, former and potential staff to get an accurate picture
- If you do not know why staff are leaving how can you prevent others going?
- A range of assessments and measurements should be used – attitude surveys, absence rates, information from career development interviews, exit interviews/questionnaires, talent audits, benchmarking, risk analysis, staff turnover rates and stability and retention rates
- Exit interviews and questionnaires are popular but are not totally reliable.

Why do some staff leave and some stay?

Today we will examine:

- Why staff leave
- Why staff stay
- Motivation and job satisfaction

Why staff leave

It is important to ask why staff leave voluntarily because if you understand the causes then you can take action to prevent others from going. Some of the assessment methods that we looked at in Monday will be useful. Reasons for leaving may be both internal and external to the organisation and can vary between staff groups and individuals who have different needs. External factors, including skills shortages in the labour market and cost of living in large cities, can be more difficult to control. Internal factors are easier to control and to rectify but managers must face up to the causes/problems. Reasons for leaving can also be looked at as push and pull factors. Push factors are internal to the organisation, usually centre on dissatisfaction, and include things like induction crisis, work pressures, work changes and leaving to avoid conflict. Pull factors are attractions outside the organisation, such as increased pay, career opportunities, promotion or a more attractive job.

Usually, there are several different complex and inter-related factors as to why staff leave and they vary in significance between individuals and staff groups. Staff who are

dissatisfied and uncommitted are more likely to leave. The most important thing is to establish the reasons for leaving, then decide on a course of action. We shall now consider some of the following factors in greater detail:

- Organisational policies and procedures
- Recruitment and selection
- Training and development
- Job satisfaction
- Appraisal, feedback and recognition
- Career development and promotion
- Money, rewards and benefits
- Stress
- Management and supervision
- Relationships with others
- Personal, health and domestic
- External

Organisational policies and procedures
Inconsistent and poor human resource policies, practices and procedures, an organisation's values, culture and climate,

organisational changes and turbulence, and poor communication can all be reasons for staff leaving. People policies need to match the organisation's culture and values. Organisations may experience difficulties because of their size or type. Small organisations may be unable to match rates of pay or promotion opportunities offered by large organisations while government/public sector organisations have difficulties matching conditions in commercial organisations. Mergers and acquisitions can negatively impact on retention due to differences in cultures, increased competition for senior positions, changes in organisations identify and poor communication prior to the merger and acquisition. In general, the employment relationship and psychological contract are important factors.

Recruitment and selection
If there are difficulties in finding new staff and/or skills shortages, some employers may appoint staff who are not suitable and who leave quickly. If honest and accurate

information or a realistic preview of the job is not provided or expectations are unfulfilled, then staff may also leave. Staff turnover can be caused by failing to match staff to the right job, so that their skills and experience are not used effectively; inadequate selection procedures; appointing the wrong person; recruiting over qualified staff; or recruiting too many exceptional staff all of whom cannot be provided with promotion opportunities.

Training and development
This is important for induction, reinforcing work culture and skills training. New staff need a proper induction not just to learn the job but to fit in with other staff and the organisation. Training and development are needed to develop teams (and in preparation for promotion) and requires support of managers/team leaders. Lack of induction, inadequate or poor training and development are all reasons for leaving. Irrelevant training is a waste of time, money and resources and potentially demotivating for the individual.

Job satisfaction
This can be a difficult term to define and means different things for individuals. Generally it refers to the job itself, the working conditions and environment and the people, as well as rewards. It makes little difference whether the job is skilled or unskilled, as many staff are influenced by the same things:

- Lack of challenging opportunities – does not stretch capability, boring job, repetitive work, lack of variety, poor job design or too little work
- Too many tasks, too much work and insufficient time
- Job too difficult/too demanding
- Abilities, skills and talents not being used effectively

- Lack of autonomy, responsibility and control over tasks
- Lack of job security
- Working with poorly trained staff or poor equipment.

Working hours can also be a source of dissatisfaction for some staff. Work environment and conditions includes many different things – a place to go during breaks, safe and healthy work conditions – and may show up as a problem, with accidents, sickness and absence, before staff leave.

Appraisal, feedback and recognition
These have implications for managers and team leaders and the way they deal with their staff. Lack of feedback, recognition or evaluation of performance, feeling undervalued or not valued at all and feeling that one's efforts are not appreciated are all problem areas. Appraisals are strongly linked to staff retention, performance and morale, and no appraisal or a poorly conducted appraisal can cause staff to leave.

Career development and promotion
Lack of personal and career development, promotion opportunities and advancement are often stated as reasons why staff leave as their aspirations are unfulfilled. Many staff see the world as their employment market and opportunity for career development and are no longer loyal to one organisation. Career progression may be slow, causing staff to seek promotion opportunities elsewhere, particularly as flatter organisations provide fewer vertical opportunities. Additionally, in lean organisations, some staff may find themselves the only one in a particular job with managers reluctant to develop or move them due to operational difficulties. This, together with a lack of interest from managers and a view that career management is the responsibility of the individual can encourage staff to leave.

Staff often comment about equity and fairness of promotion and their relationship with those responsible for promotion. Career development should be linked to appraisal/performance management and career counselling. Inappropriate career systems, lack of training and development that would enable individuals to be considered for promotion and inconsistency between different managers can all be areas of frustration.

Money, rewards and benefits
Money is rarely the only reason why staff leave – it is usually part of a bigger problem. Even if potential leavers are offered more money to stay, they are unlikely to. Many staff earning large amounts of money are unhappy in their jobs while staff earning less can be very happy. Having said that, it is unusual for staff to leave for less money and they often secure higher compensation packages with a different employer. Those staying and those leaving both complain about money and rewards, but leavers frequently comment that they are poorly paid and not paid enough to satisfy their needs. Employers need to consider cost of living and cost of housing, which can vary by region, whether pay is low when compared with competitors, and potential inequities. As well as money, inequitable and unfair benefits and reward systems can be a source of dissatisfaction.

Stress
This is a reason for some staff leaving. Some stress can be useful, but long-term problems can occur. You should consider:

- What work issues could cause long lasting and high levels of stress? Poor selection, lack of relevant training and development, bullying and harassment, lack of knowledge/skills and competence, unrealistic time pressures and deadlines, boring work, lack of managerial support, ineffective senior management, too few staff, poor relationships with others, high turnover of staff, organisational culture, poor communications, ambiguity, lack of control, customers/clients, noise, lighting, ergonomics, conflict between personal life and work

- Which staff are more susceptible to stress? Some causes of stress are individually based and self inflicted – poor time management, lack of prioritising
- Which staff are unlikely or unable to cope with pressure?
- Whether managers and others are doing enough to prevent stress?
- The signs of stress – headaches, stomach aches, backaches, crying, tension, short tempered, irritable, argumentative, making mistakes, no enthusiasm, easily upset, no energy, tiredness, worrying, not sleeping, depression, anger, compulsive eating, inflexibility, irrational, unable to relax
- The causes of stress and take necessary action.

Management and supervision

Managers and team leaders can be the cause of staff leaving. Traditional management approaches are unlikely to work for staff who are working remotely. Many managers lack basic practical leadership skills leading to poor individual and organisation performance. Additionally, they lack interpersonal skills, are poor communicators and have difficulty leading teams, motivating people and developing ethical standards. Some manage by punishment and not by reward and praise because they know no better. Relationships and management style are therefore critical to job satisfaction and retention. Staff leave managers not organisations and often would rather work for good managers in poor organisations than poor managers in good organisations. Weak, incompetent and poor-quality managers who abdicate their responsibilities, are disinterested in staff, do not develop them, are unfair and unequal are significant factors. You need to ask whether managers care about their staff, design their jobs appropriately and use their staff effectively, or whether they make poor recruitment and selection decisions, provide poor induction, little training and development and are costing the organisation money because of poor staff retention. Examine exit interviews for comments, and consider whether specific managers experience greater turnover than others and if there are more requests for transfers from certain departments. Conflicts between managers and staff do occur and can result in poor relationships partly because of management style and personality. Lack of support and feedback, lack of direction, particularly regarding performance targets and objectives, being unapproachable and having poor communication can cause staff to leave. Staff have expectations about loyalty, trust, feedback, support and interesting work from their managers/team leaders. They do not expect to be treated unfairly, abused, bullied or harassed.

Relationships with others
As well as relationships with managers and team leaders, staff nearly always work with others. Some prefer to work alone and some like to be with other staff. If their preference is not matched or if they have poor relationships or conflict, they may leave.

Personal, health and domestic
As well as stress, staff often state the balance between work and their personal lives as reasons for leaving. Circumstances, responsibilities and commitments, especially concerning family, may result in some individuals wanting more contact with their families or more personal life. Working hours, such as long

hours, shift working and lack of flexibility, can cause problems. Working away from home for long periods of time can make it difficult to plan a personal life. Working overseas, either short-term or semi-permanently, excessive business travel and travelling difficulties to work are all important factors. Other personal reasons include pregnancy, health, medical, return to education and relocation, as well as cost of living and housing.

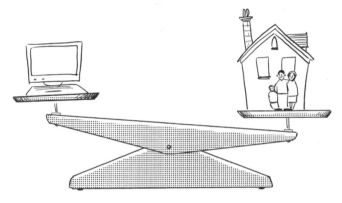

External

The external environment, such as a strong economic situation, may provide lots of opportunities for staff wanting more experience or a change of job. Staff may be head-hunted by other organisations.

Why staff stay

What staff want from their jobs and why they stay will potentially vary between individuals, teams/groups, team leaders and managers. The reasons why some staff stay can be the cause of others leaving. They often stay because they are motivated and have job satisfaction. Why staff stay is dependant upon a number of factors:

- Economic problems, afraid to change and too much to lose
- Good pay, benefits and conditions – bonuses, overtime, holidays, pension, car, child care provision
- Job security and stability
- Regular convenient working hours, flexible hours
- Career development and advancement opportunities
- Good training and development opportunities; able to expand knowledge and learn new skills
- Coaching and counselling from manager or team leader
- Good relationship with colleagues and managers
- Fair, competent and effective management
- Supportive environment, sense of belonging, inclusion and therefore a potential loss of friendships. Fun place to work
- Able to work in a team or work alone as required
- Respected as an individual and as a professional
- Able to manage, supervise or influence others
- Convenient location/easy to get to work
- Age (close to retirement)
- Good working environment and conditions with current equipment and modern practices
- Clear goals, objectives and expectations
- Interesting, varied and challenging work; able to use skills and abilities effectively
- Appropriate and realistic workload
- Effective two way communication
- Contribution recognised, appreciated and rewarded either individually or in a team; feedback and appraisal given
- Personal/professional autonomy and freedom; able to make decisions and solve problems; able to explore new ideas and be creative
- Size of organisation – smaller organisations can often offer greater autonomy, more challenging and meaningful

work, opportunities for development; larger organisations can offer promotion and development opportunities
- Associated with a reputable, ethical organisation – loyalty and commitment to the organisation's values
- Organisation has a clear sense of direction.

Motivation and job satisfaction

There is a strong relationship between motivation, job satisfaction and commitment, and intention to leave, staff turnover and retention. If needs are met, it can prevent staff turnover and increase retention. However, when staff are not motivated there may be some obvious signs. Those with responsibility for staff need to be aware of what these signs are and take action if they see evidence of:

- Absenteeism and high staff turnover
- Poor time-keeping and wasting time – arriving late, leaving early
- Poor working relationships, lack of co-operation, complaints from customers, colleagues, managers
- Poor performance and standard of work, not achieving targets or deadlines, making mistakes, and unacceptable pace of work. Failure to carry out instructions
- Irritability, stress, poor commitment and low morale
- Discipline problems
- Wasted talent.

Individual differences and needs will influence whether staff are satisfied or not. Managers and team leaders must understand these differences and identify the things that motivate and de-motivate staff and understand how they relate to staff retention.

There are lots of theories of motivation but we do not have time to deal with them this week but you should remember that motivation deals with various needs. Basic needs that explain why people work and what makes people work harder and look for more, include: achievement and recognition, pay, sense of belonging, able to work with other people, healthy working environment, good working conditions, able to contribute, make decisions and use abilities effectively. These form the basis of most theories of motivation. Money can motivate, but only for those people who are motivated by money.

If staff are unhappy they will weigh up the advantages and disadvantages of staying or leaving. This will vary for individuals. Managers and others with responsibility for staff need to ensure that the reasons for staying are stronger than the reasons for going for staff they want to keep and recognise that they can do something about staff turnover and retention. If no action is taken, staff turnover can become self-perpetuating.

Summary

So now we know something about the reasons why some staff leave and some stay:

- Many different factors contribute to staff leaving or staying
- The factors that cause some staff to leave are the same factors that make others stay
- Managers and others with responsibility for staff must understand that staff are different and have different needs
- Motivation and job satisfaction varies between individuals.

How to keep staff now

Today we will examine:

- How to keep staff now
- Short-term strategies

Any staff retention strategy should aim to keep the staff that an organisation wants, by satisfying their needs, and to reduce the number of staff recruited as this is costly and time consuming. Employers need to analyse and understand the causes of staff turnover before putting in place solutions to encourage staff retention. You will therefore need to use some of the methods we discussed in Monday. Do not jump to conclusions and make assumptions as you might come up with the wrong solutions. Solutions can take many different forms and do not necessarily have to be expensive or incur additional costs in order to have benefits for the individual and the organisation. Employers need to know what staff turnover is costing and how much they are losing before deciding how much they are prepared to invest in keeping staff.

How to keep staff now

Trying to persuade staff to stay once they have resigned is really too late. Counter offers, such as more money, are rarely successful but if staff are worth keeping then you can try persuading them to stay. You need to compare the costs of them going with the costs of them staying (not just financial costs) and consider whether it will have an adverse effect on the rest of the organisation if they leave. You can use extended notice periods to allow staff to think, reflect and possibly change their mind. Watch out for staff who are considering leaving; the ones who do not commit themselves to long-term projects, have a change of attitude, do not care, distance themselves, do not communicate, have odd days off, want holidays at short notice or make secretive phonecalls. You may be able to prevent them leaving. If good staff leave, tell them that they can come back. Contact them after they have gone and see if they will return. Their new job may not be as good as they thought. Exit questionnaires, phonecalls and personal contacts can all be used and following up after three months allows former staff time to reflect. Where there are shortages, such as nurses, bringing them back even years later can still be cost effective because they already have basic skills, know what the job involves and only need retraining or updating. If former staff do come back it can save time and money and shows existing staff that they may be better off where they are, which improves retention.

Short-term strategies

The following are short-term strategies that can improve staff retention:

- Recruitment and selection
- Induction
- Training and development
- Appraisal, feedback and recognition
- Performance
- Money, rewards and benefits

Recruitment and selection
This is time-consuming and costly but an important part of

W E D N E S D A Y

staff retention so care and attention needs to go into this stage. Good recruitment and selection means selecting excellent staff who will make a positive difference to your organisation, perhaps helping it to expand and be more profitable. Skilled people are in demand and are usually not unemployed so the organisation needs to be seen as a good place to work and have a good reputation to attract them. If there are skills shortages and recruitment difficulties, avoid appointing people who do not fully match the criteria, however tempting this may be. They will only add to your staff turnover problems. So, how do you attract, select and appoint the right people in the first place, those who will wish to stay with the organisation? Consider the following points:

- Where you recruit from and what factors are likely to attract or deter people from joining the organisation. If the organisation has a reputation as a good employer – honest and fair – then it is more likely to attract and retain staff. If there are no applicants it may be because of skills shortages or organisation's reputation
- If you want to employ ethical staff then the organisation has to be ethical. Managers and staff should be role models and be ethical, trustworthy, honest, moral, law-abiding and giving and earning respect
- Skills for the job should be clearly specified and the job accurately described so staff selected are neither over- nor under-skilled with a good fit between person and job
- Advertisements and literature should be realistic and accurate and include details of pay and working arrangements to attract candidates. If you want lots of experience and qualifications then this should match pay offered

- Examine why candidates left their previous job. If they have lots of job changes then they may add to your staff retention problems
- Find out early what potential staff want, what will keep them happy and whether you can meet their expectations. What do you promise potential staff and can you fulfil the promises? If you can't match their expectations you will only add to retention difficulties
- Recruitment and selection is a two-way process. Provide accurate information so both parties can make a decision about whether to offer/accept job. An honest and realistic view of the job should be provided. This helps with commitment and loyalty
- Recruit staff who believe in the organisation's values
- Use a variety of selection methods – testing, interviews, assessments, simulations, group problem-solving activities, work sampling, demonstration of skills, assessment centres, references (especially former employers)
- Those involved in recruitment and selection need training
- Use team members in recruitment. They have some ownership of the process, feel more responsible for new staff and new staff are more likely to stay
- During interviews do candidates lack enthusiasm, are they critical about former organisation/colleagues, do they appear over qualified, are they interested in the job?
- How do you deal with unsuccessful candidates? You may wish to consider them in the future
- Constantly evaluate recruitment and selection methods. Think about changes you might need to make – using head-hunters, recruitment agencies
- Recruiting and selecting new/temporary staff has an effect upon existing employees.

Induction

This is vital to ensure a sense of belonging and is necessary
for every member of staff regardless of their position. It helps
new staff learn organisational values, perform more
effectively and stay with the organisation. It requires:

- Time – more than just the first day or a few hours
- Equipment and resources
- Opportunities to meet and work with new colleagues
- A buddy, replaced later by a coach or mentor
- Clear objectives and criteria for performance
- Learning and training – not just showing someone how to
  do things
- The creation of a development plan
- Opportunity to succeed and feel satisfied
- Discussions with manager, including feedback and
  review
- Demonstration by managers and team leaders that they are
  committed to new staff and support induction.

Induction should reflect what it's like to work in the organisation. How do new staff feel at the end of the first day, first week, first month, or have they already left? Induction should be provided for existing staff who are promoted or change jobs or departments. A good induction can help retain staff and avoid induction crisis.

Training and development
This helps transmit the culture and values of an organisation, can reduce turnover, encourage retention and create a more stable workforce. It can also improve performance, reduce errors/mistakes and absenteeism, improve job satisfaction and can be seen as a reward in its own right. Learning, training and development can help attract and retain people and develop commitment, skills, competence and adaptability. You should:

- Develop an organisational training and development strategy covering induction, initial training, continuous training and development, preparation for change, career development, performance improvement and management development. A long term view is required
- Implement, review and evaluate strategy; ensure adequate resources are available including e-learning, action and project based learning
- Encourage regular learning and development activities for everyone, both job and non-job related; this maintains interest, promotes learning and increases job satisfaction when promotion opportunities are limited
- Encourage management training and development and executive coaching
- Allow staff to train and develop others
- Develop a supportive environment in which team leaders and managers have time to listen, encourage development and

provide mentoring and coaching. Mentoring and coaching can provide the link between recruitment and retention

- Support individual training and provide opportunities for self-development and continuous learning
- Provide specialised training and development and multi-skilling; this provides new interests and enables organisations to cope with additional work; also improves flexibility and versatility in an ever changing workplace and can help internal career development and promotion
- Consider where skills shortages exist, train and develop your own staff and consider how to retain apprentices
- Give staff working from home and those on career breaks training and development. Provide child care if necessary to enable staff to attend courses
- Involve staff in planning their own learning and training and encourage them to learn from mistakes
- Provide skills updating, product knowledge, technical training and interpersonal skills. Allow staff to use their new skills and knowledge
- Recognise that professional staff need continuous professional development.

Training and development can be a strong satisfier helping to prepare staff for change and the future. There appears to be a link between training and development and staff retention.

Appraisal, feedback and recognition
Regular feedback and recognition through reviews and appraisals, as well as on a daily basis, are important for motivation, commitment and staff retention. Feedback needs to be given about good things as well as areas for improvement. Use appraisals/reviews to motivate, set realistic and achievable goals and deadlines. Praise staff

openly: be prepared to write letters of congratulation (or arrange for senior managers to do so) and publicise achievements in newsletters, on notice boards or by e-mail.

Performance

Managers and team leaders must deal with poor performance and if necessary remove poor performers from the organisation as they create additional responsibilities and difficulties for colleagues and can have a negative effect upon good staff. Remember that getting rid of poorly performing staff can be costly but organisations should not tolerate poor performance. Managers need to know their staff and build their confidence and abilities, in order that they perform effectively and contribute to the productivity of the department and organisation. Staff need a number of things in order to perform well and this links to staff retention. They need:

- Knowledge, skills, competencies via training, instruction, practice, feedback, assessment
- Safe and healthy working environment
- Support from colleagues, team members, managers
- Constructive, specific and honest feedback together with praise and rewards – financial and non-financial
- Well-designed jobs, resources and equipment
- Clear standards of performance and opportunities to discuss performance.

Simply being present or working long hours does not equal effective performance. Effective performance needs competent staff who have been properly recruited, inducted and trained. They should have the knowledge, skills, abilities and capabilities to do the job effectively, be motivated and be regularly assessed.

Money, rewards and benefits

Managing rewards and benefits can attract, motivate and retain staff. Reward policies and strategies need to sit comfortably with the internal and external environment, reflect the organisation's values and beliefs. They should support organisational objectives and be integrated with other people policies. Rewards and benefits can be financial or non-financial and are influenced by systems, cultural factors (national and organisational), economic issues (labour markets, supply and demand, local pay rates/structure), as well as by motivation theories. Rewards and benefits apply as follows:

- Individual – basic salary with possibility of additional rewards for performance, achievement and individual contribution. Individual benefits do not necessarily increase knowledge, team working or reinforce what the organisation wants
- Team – based on team achieving its targets/objectives; team rewards should reinforce team-working culture
- Organisation – based on organisation performance and achievement of targets; usually cash, shares or profit-related.

You also need to consider the following points:

- Review rates of pay. Use benchmarking, information from exit interviews and any other sources. Are your salaries competitive and appropriate for your staff?
- Rewards need to be fair, equitable, realistic, transparent and consistent as well as appropriate. Criteria should be clear so staff know how they can obtain them
- Remember rewards cannot be given for everything but should be made when staff have performed exceptionally well or if you want to reinforce something

- Rewards should match and reinforce what an organisation wants. If a focus on people is required, then managers should be measured and rewarded on people issues not profits, financial results and technical competence
- Rewards should be made quickly. Delays can de-motivate
- Rewards depend upon organisational policies, opportunities for promotion and money/resources available
- Not all rewards are costly; be creative and think about what staff would like and what can be offered. Thanks, praise and recognition are important and cost nothing
- Flexible benefits provide a choice; staff surveys and effective communication are required to determine what benefits staff want, what they would like to change and to ensure staff know what benefits are on offer
- On-line benefits are easier to adminster and to determine who is using which benefits either individually or by groups
- Staff vary by age, family responsibilities and lifestyle so requirements differ. Allow staff to trade salaries against other benefits such as additional holidays, childcare vouchers or healthcare
- Financial and non-financial rewards are difficult to differentiate as some non-financial rewards have a financial value and staff should be made aware of their value
- Retention bonuses reward staff for staying and attempt to prevent them leaving. They do not deal with causes of staff turnover and are not always successful
- What rewards are you going to offer in the future?

The following is a list of many possible rewards, both financial and non-financial.

Recognition Special bonuses for exceptional performance – holiday, time off, long service dinners/awards Free birthday cakes Lunch with the MD/CEO for outstanding staff or long service Letter of thanks, certificates Employee of the month – photo, day off, staff newsletter, badge Points/award programmes Small gift – chocolates, wine	**Holidays/Working hours** Holiday/annual leave Additional holidays Extended parental leave Early finish on Fridays, long week-ends and summer working hours Flexible working/variable hours/job share Flexible retirement age Time off for working late Compassionate leave for emergencies
Pay & financial Competitive basic pay/salary Financial loans Incremental pay increases and cost of living Payment of professional fees Stock/share options Pensions Profit related pay Long service pay Pay for overtime, on-call, premium and extra hours Performance related pay, payment by results and by hours worked Cash bonuses (calendar & project based) and commission Payment for recommending and recruiting a friend	**Health** On site health care, doctors, dentists, health screening, vaccinations, counselling Private medical/dental insurance Specific health care to cover male and female cancers Discount on healthcare if not offered by employer Sick pay schemes Sports/leisure facilities for staff and family Subsidised personal trainer Well-being centres – yoga, massage, aromatherapy Bicycles to travel to work and use at lunchtime Life assurance
Retention and loyalty bonuses Golden Hellos Golden handcuffs Retention bonuses if stay another year	**Secondments** Gap year for executives/mature staff Sabbaticals Unpaid career breaks
Social Parties for staff, partners, family and children – Christmas, summer balls and barbecues Helicopter/hot air balloon trips Snooker tables in the office	**Travel** Working abroad/business travel Travel/holiday packages or vouchers Travel insurance Taking partner on business trip

Time to watch sporting events Dress down/casual dress Go-karting Clubs for travel, film, theatre, wine, football, athletics, sailing	Weekends abroad with partner and subsidised holidays Free flights/hotels Banking/currency
Training & development Learning opportunities and training courses Professionally accredited courses Technical/Management training Open learning centres/library – business and personal use External conferences/seminars Retirement planning/training Costs of external courses and support for degrees Access to e-learning Personal effectiveness courses	**Child/Family** Childcare/nurseries Parental/adoption leave and time for fertility treatment Emergency back-up child care Grandparent leave for older staff Additional maternity and paternity leave opportunity to work from home Family days – take parents/children to work Christmas presents for children
Computers Free access to computers, Internet and e-learning packages for personal use Discounts on computers PC leasing scheme for home use	**Team activities** Team/staff day out Involved in a special team/project Cross country rallying and 4 wheel drive expeditions Outdoor/adventure courses
Food Free coffee, meals, fruit Subsidised canteen, luncheon vouchers Champagne and pizzas or free meals for working late, free drinks in local pub Easter eggs for staff Christmas hampers and turkeys	**Other services** On line/telephone concierge & valet services Groceries/shopping delivered to workplace Legal advice/legal helpline Ironing service On-site food, petrol, shopping, dry cleaning, car cleaning
Community Voluntary work Time off as volunteer – reserve armed forces Leave for community, charitable and voluntary work – monthly or annual allowance	**Housing/accommodation** Mortgage subsidy or loans for housing Subsidised housing, rent or accommodation; relocation costs Holiday homes – free or subsidised Use of van to move house Additional leave for moving house

Other benefits	Other benefits
Parking space	Telephone bills/Mobile phones
Free tickets to corporate events	Tickets for theatre, football
Duvet days	Car or allowance, hire car
Presents and gifts	Discounts on products/services
Renting a cinema for staff and	Status, job title, own office
family for the release of new film	Major organisational product
Retail vouchers for high street	given away each month
stores and catalogue gifts	Taking pets to work/help with
Uniform/clothing alowance	vet's bills

Be careful. While providing lots of benefits can help staff retention, it can also encourage staff to work more hours and stay at work longer. This can have consequences for work-life balance.

Summary

So now we know something about how to keep staff and what we can do short-term.

- Try to prevent good staff leaving and if they do leave, contact them once they have gone and encourage them to come back
- Attract and select good people in the first place to improve staff retention
- Provide induction for all staff and encourage training and development
- Provide feedback on performance both formally through appraisal and informally on a daily basis if necessary
- Offer a variety of rewards and benefits to satisfy individual needs
- Accept that some staff will leave.

How to keep staff in the future

Today, we will examine:

- Long-term strategies
- Reviewing and assessing retention strategies

Long-term strategies

It is not always easy to differentiate between short- and long-term strategies as these will vary between organisations depending on how significant the causes are and therefore how quickly solutions have to be implemented. We can consider the following long-term:

- Job design
- Personal/work life balance
- Career development and promotion
- Talent management
- Job satisfaction
- Motivation
- Stress
- Management and supervision
- Relationships with others
- Communication
- Work environment
- Decision-making and involvement
- Innovation and creativity
- Organisational policies, practices and procedures
- Organisations – culture, values, size and structure
- Human resource planning

Job design

This is concerned with the content of jobs and is important to both the individual and the organisation. Job design or redesign can lead to improvements in productivity, performance, job satisfaction and staff retention. The need for redesign can be caused by:

- Poor performance and staff retention problems
- Changes in the organisation, including use of technology, team-working and management practice
- Organisation's culture and structure
- Physical working conditions/environment
- Position within the organisation – permanent or temporary
- Salaries, benefits and rewards.

While there can be difficulties introducing such changes because of equipment, machinery, resources, and the constraints of meeting customer expectations or financial targets, it can help accommodate individual differences and needs. Practical job design or redesign includes:

- Job enlargement – adding different tasks to create variety and interest; associated with horizontal growth
- Job enrichment – making jobs more interesting, challenging and providing growth for the person by increasing responsibility, removing management control, introducing new, more difficult and sometimes more specialised tasks; associated with vertical growth
- Job rotation – doing different jobs to increase variety especially when jobs/tasks are boring or repetitive
- Self-managed teams or autonomous groups – team/group responsible for tasks, jobs and managing activities
- Job-sharing and different working patterns.

Personal/work life balance

Some staff and employers are becoming more concerned about the effects of work on health and individual lives. Recognition of the problem and doing something about it should enable staff to balance their working and personal lives more easily. Some employers are providing additional facilities at work as well as trying to be more flexible in accommodating the needs of staff. There are several different and flexible working arrangements:

- Part-time, shorter hours and seasonal work
- Flexitime – choice of starting and finishing times
- Flexible working hours/compressed working weeks
- Home working and telecommuting
- Term time working – right to paid or unpaid leave during school holidays without contract ending
- Annualised hours – total hours worked in a year. Weekly hours can vary
- Career breaks and unpaid leave
- Job-sharing, where one job, salary and benefits are shared between two staff on a part-time basis, either by day, week, part-week or alternate weeks.

Flexibility is based on trust and responsibility and relates to the culture of the organisation. Focusing on work life balance, including different and flexible working arrangements, can improve morale and productivity, reduce absenteeism and staff turnover. You should:

- Acknowledge staff working too many hours and discourage them from simply being at work. Focus on outcomes and productivity and if necessary tell them to go home
- Examine what shift working and other arrangements mean for work life balance, social activities, sports and hobbies

- Provide healthy food in canteens and consider free meals for those working long hours
- Have arrangements (paid or unpaid) for emergencies and special circumstances
- Encourage staff to get involved with voluntary projects and give something to the community
- Ensure that if you provide leisure, health or shopping facilities at work that this aids retention and does not keep staff at work. Ensure that such facilities are available to all staff
- Managers need to be proactive about work life balance. It rarely happens without a positive approach and leadership.

Particularly when there are skills shortages, some staff (or potential staff) do not wish to relocate. However, providing the necessary equipment and technology can enable many to work from home or from anywhere in the world. Remote and home workers need the support of the IT department if they are to work effectively and perhaps also a second phone line and office equipment. Allowing staff freedom in the way they work and where they work demonstrates trust and can help retention.

Career development and promotion

Many organisations have limited opportunities for vertical promotion. A career can mean different things to people: it may not necessarily involve the same job, profession or same sector or even involve promotion, however, the lack of career advancement opportunities can cause some staff to leave. For those individuals seeking career development, employers need to be creative, provide development opportunities and offer other experiences. New and different career paths are required and career advancement needs to be thought of more broadly with projects and team working rather than traditional upward promotion. Career development is an individual responsibility but staff who see a future with an organisation are more likely to stay. Staff who are promoted can act as role models for others and improve commitment; promotion is seen as a reward. You should:

- Talk to staff about what they want, assist with objective setting and personal goals and try to help staff achieve them
- Promote from within where appropriate as this can reduce staff turnover, improve motivation and morale, reduce costs and increase staff retention
- Consider horizontal and vertical positions for promotion, development and challenge
- Provide training for managers and team leaders, who need skills in mentoring, coaching and facilitation
- Examine how internal jobs are advertised including use of intranet, databases, online job shops, secondment and project opportunities
- Make it easy for staff to transfer internally – benefits the organisation as a whole

- Find further challenging assignments including opportunities to join project teams
- Examine promotion criteria to ensure equity and fairness
- Examine career development strategies and adopt a variety of approaches including career paths
- Consider links with appraisal, performance management and feedback – assessment of performance is linked with career development for those seeking progression.

Talent management
Those identified with high potential and talent need specific management.

- Identify staff with potential by assessing skills and abilities. Identified talent are those that an organisation wants to keep and invest in
- Talented staff look for clear strategy, challenging tasks, rewards based on organisation performance and a lack of bureaucracy
- Talented staff need jobs that stretch them. New job assignments, cross functional moves, profit & loss responsibility, chance to start a new business activity, member of high profile working parties, overseas assignments, temporary assignments, personal development/time for course work, attendance at conferences so they can develop skills and grow
- Ensure expertise exists in mentoring, coaching and feedback
- Appoint mentors, create personal development plans and provide development opportunities early
- Consider what training and development is required in preparation for next role or promotion. This requires a training and career development strategy
- Talented staff should be promoted quickly. They can move more than one grade at a time

- Training and development should broaden experience and help build individual and organisational capability
- Talented staff should be viewed as organisation, not department or business unit talent
- Consider what additional rewards and responsibilities staff receive upon completion of educational programmes
- Ensure talent is used effectively. Staff become frustrated and demotivated when their skills are not used. Wasted talent can cause organisations to under perform
- The greatest staff turnover can occur in talented and high potential staff. Consider investment versus turnover
- Focusing on talented staff can de-motivate others. What can be done to make them feel valued and stay?

Job satisfaction

Staff often enjoy their jobs if they are able to use their skills and abilities and have opportunities for development. Money and rewards do not necessarily motivate them. Job satisfaction relies on a number of things:

- The workplace has to be a positive place and must *feel good* to be there; for some it also has to be a fun place to work
- Job satisfaction is complex and involves management, colleagues, job, working conditions and environment, pay and rewards, job design
- Staff encouraged to put forward ideas, make decisions, have control over their work and understand how they contribute to the organisation
- An open culture and staff consultation improves communication and job satisfaction; existing culture may need to be changed
- Work environment should be safe and healthy. Health care provision shows staff that they are valued

- Work should be challenging and encourage improvement in performance and personal growth; challenging work provides job satisfaction and links to career development
- Staff should be encouraged to work in and work with staff from different departments for growth and development
- Clear reporting lines in complex organisational structures
- Adequate resources must be provided
- Creativity and innovation should be encouraged
- Job content and design must be examined and regularly reviewed. Ensure that job descriptions do not restrict, that there is variety, challenge and responsibility; make jobs more interesting and challenging not just bigger
- Job rotation and special assignments to overcome boredom and make work more interesting
- Job and member of staff should be accurately matched.

Motivation

Managers and team leaders need to know what motivates staff, then motivate and reward them appropriately. They need to have a positive influence on staff, encouraging them to work and to perform better. Guidelines for motivating staff include the following, some of which we have already considered:

- Recognising individual needs of staff
- Communication, particularly listening
- Challenging, interesting and responsible tasks
- Asking for opinions and involving in decision-making
- Setting realistic targets
- Praising and rewarding when targets are achieved
- Providing recognition and feedback
- Informing staff of the value of their contribution
- Giving staff sufficient autonomy
- Being a good role model yourself.

Motivation can also be improved by an effective appraisal and performance management system, job redesign and organisation design, in terms of its structure, lines of communication and decision-making. Managers and team leaders need to motivate positively using incentives and rewards rather than fear and threats and recognise that there may be differences between full-time permanent staff and others who are part-time or temporary.

Stress
Symptoms of stress, such as physical signs, absenteeism, lack of motivation and apathy, need to be recognised and dealt with. The causes of stress need to be understood and prevented by providing extra staff, extra time and ensuring pressure is only ever short term, not long term.

Management and supervision
Managers and team leaders have a significant role in preventing staff turnover and retaining staff. They need to be effective in a number of different ways. We shall look in detail at their roles in Saturday.

Relationships with others

Staff have individual needs. Some prefer to work alone while others need to work in an effective team. Most organisations rely on teams at some time so managers need to build and develop teams and ensure that the needs of individuals are considered. Conflicts will also need to be resolved.

Communication

Managers need to engage in effective communication, recognising that communication is a two-way process. Remember the following points:

- Staff need frequent formal and informal communication. Consider weekly e-mails, quarterly meetings with senior management, monthly company magazines, Chief Executive/Managing Director presentations
- Communicate and share information about business plans, strategy, goals, vision and mission
- Use a variety of communication methods – notice boards, group/team meetings, electronic media, e-mail, intranets, newsletters, one-to-one contact, videos, conferences
- Listen to all staff, including those who leave. Ask for and implement staff suggestions and ask for their advice
- Effective communication will help you understand your staff and their needs. Communication should focus on individuals in terms of objectives, performance, feedback, praise, consultation and discussion
- Staff forums can be effective for suggestions, raising issues and general communication. Focus groups and surveys can be used to determine staff views and discuss policies
- Chief Executives, Managing Directors and Senior Managers are crucial to the communication process. They need to be accessible, visit staff regularly and experience

the jobs their staff do to keep in touch. Hosting breakfast or lunch meetings with randomly selected staff to ask for their opinions can be useful. Consider access to the senior management team by e-mail and sharing important director and senior managers meetings by video. A real open door policy can be the key to respect and retention

- Regular department or team meetings encourages feedback and communication. Team building activities and out of office retreats can also help
- Open communications should reflect culture. Inform staff of issues both good and bad and share financial information
- Open plan offices where everyone sits together, one canteen and no special car parking spaces helps break down barriers, aids communication and creates a sense of community
- Knowing everyone by their first name also helps
- When there are major changes, mergers and acquisitions communicate regularly and honestly.

Work environment
The physical working environment can be important to staff retention and helps communication and stress reduction. A number of different things are possible:

- Open plan layout with staff and managers able to sit with colleagues and project teams. No executive offices, office doors and secretaries to hide behind
- Relaxation areas. Sofas in coffee areas, gardens, chill out areas with tropical fish, plants and comfortable seating. TV's in certain areas
- In large organisations, a community feel with shops, banks and coffee shops
- Fresh air pumped into buildings with adequate ventilation and natural light to avoid sick building syndrome.

Decision-making and involvement
Staff that are actively involved in an organisation are less
likely to leave it.

- Involve staff in decision-making, particularly decisions that
  affect them and their work. This helps overcomes resistance
  to change, increases commitment, sense of belonging and
  ownership and can improve performance and productivity
- Ask staff for their views and ideas both formally and
  informally. Suggestion schemes can aid competitive
  advantage and staff retention and reward staff. Initially, it
  requires effective communication of organisational
  problems and areas for improvement
- Consult with staff and have open discussions.

Innovation and creativity
For organisations to prosper they need to foster innovation
and creativity.

- Create a 'can do' culture that supports creativity and
  ensure values, processes and behaviours are aligned. Do
  not accept complacency
- Build effective teams and ensure they have the right skills
  and behaviours. Provide honest and timely feedback and
  encourage creative teamwork
- Develop visionary leadership and leadership qualities
- Encourage creativity and fresh thinking
- Provide resources to convert creativity into outcomes and
  benefits. Reward staff for their ideas
- Keep close to staff and issues. Communicate, listen and be
  seen around the organisation
- Consider how to deal with mistakes and failure. If you
  want staff to be creative then a no blame culture and
  allowing people to learn from mistakes is important.

Organisational policies, practices and procedures
Policies and practices apply to the issues we have already
looked at, such as rewards and benefits, communication,
appraisal/performance management, equity and fairness,
working conditions, hours of work, training and
development. No single strategy will work and a combination
of strategies will most probably be required. People policies
and practices need to be integrated with other organisational
practices, strategy, structure and processes and should
enhance the image and reflect the culture of the organisation.
Policies and practices are influential in attracting and
retaining talented quality staff and employers need to devise
attractive employment initiatives and be more strategic about
people. Employers need to consider the importance of new
employment contracts that encourage flexibility and
responsibility in comparison to traditional contracts and
policies whilst observing the legal framework of the country
in which they are based. Monitor equal opportunities and if
necessary increase awareness. Appropriate organisational
processes, policies and practices need to be in place, regularly
reviewed and improved.

Organisations – culture, values, size and structure
Sometimes an organisations culture, values, climate and
management attitudes/style need to be changed to increase
commitment and to ensure the success of policies and practices.
A caring approach and attitude that extends to individual,
team and family members can be key to a happy and
productive workforce. This is helped by flat open structures
and by the size of the organisation. Small organisations are
often closer to staff and resemble a small community with a
family or village like feel creating a sense of belonging.

Consider organisation size and structure. The values of an organisation are important in staff retention such as support for community, charitable, ethical and environmental projects. Relying on external recruitment does not address internal problems with structure, systems and processes nor does it aid the growth and development of internal talent. How do your staff know that they are valued and that you care?

Human resource planning
This is to do with supply and demand, long- and short-term requirements, forecasting, planning, attracting and retaining staff. It is concerned with having the right number of people with the right skills and abilities in the right place at the right time and retaining them. If future staffing needs are to be estimated reliably, then past turnover is important. Are the causes internal (policies and procedures) or external (labour market/economy)? The information needed for effective planning includes details of:

- Current staffing levels; how many staff – too many or too few? What is the age profile, likely retirements, gender, length of service, grade, current jobs, qualification and skills levels of staff?
- Recruitment – who do you need and how will you get them? What demographic changes are there, levels of unemployment and skills shortages at local, regional, national and international levels?
- Staff turnover – rates, reasons for leaving and implications?
- Staff who can be considered for internal promotion
- Pay policies and costs of staff – local, national and international rates
- Characteristics of specific groups.

This information should be accurately recorded to allow comparisons between years or groups and enable predictions to be made. Effective human resource planning ensures correct recruitment and selection, can reduce staff turnover and job dissatisfaction and improve staff retention.

Reviewing and assessing retention strategies

No single retention strategy will work for all staff in all organisations. Highly concentrated retention schemes, focusing on specific individuals or groups can be more effective then an organisation wide approach. Develop local strategies if necessary to deal with local problems. You must remember that staff are different with different needs and that organisations are also different. You need to know what is important for your staff and recognise that this may change. Respond to the needs and desires of staff where appropriate. As an employer, you need to know what the normal rates of staff turnover are for your organisation and whether they are increasing, decreasing or staying the same.

The strategies that you put in place to reduce staff turnover and retain staff need to be regularly reviewed and updated. If staff are satisfied and you have a stable workforce, then you are more likely to retain staff, have satisfied customers and a successful and profitable organisation. If you create a good place to work, are seen to be fair, treat staff consistently, have equitable policies and procedures, people will be more attracted to the organisation and staff more inclined to stay. Motivated, committed and happy staff can have a positive effect on other staff and enhance the reputation of the organisation. Use these staff to train and develop others and promote policies and practices.

Remember there are other employers out there who might like to employ your staff. You do not want to be in the position where staff are asking themselves *Do I stay or do I go?* If you want to keep them and prevent them going then you need to take action. Staff are a valuable resource – can you really afford to ignore staff retention? The success of your retention strategies can be assessed by how many of the staff you want to retain are still employed by your organisation.

Summary

Now we know something about long-term strategies, and reviewing and assessing retention strategies.

- Many different long-term strategies can be used to assist staff retention and no single strategy will work
- Work life balance is becoming increasingly important and reflects individual differences and needs
- You need to plan effectively to attract and retain staff
- Policies, practices, procedures and retention strategies should be regularly reviewed and assessed.

Pros and cons of staff retention

Today, we will be looking at:

- Specific groups of people
- The benefits of staff retention
- The disadvantages of staff retention and advantages of staff turnover
- The costs of staff turnover
- The costs of staff retention

Specific groups of people

Those with responsibility for staff retention need to look at specific groups and understand what individuals want as this will vary by age, gender, during their careers (early, mid and late career) and as their lives change. Variations can exist between professions, levels, industries and sectors as well as between cultures and nationalities. Individual retention strategies are almost needed.

- Parents
- Women
- Men
- Young people/school leavers
- Graduates
- Older workers
- Senior managers/professionals
- Specialist skills areas
- Low skilled staff
- Call centre staff

Parents

Offering family-friendly policies, such as part-time working, job-sharing, home-working, flexitime and subsidised nurseries, can have benefits in improved staff commitment and motivation, job satisfaction, absence rates, productivity, quality of work, recruitment and staff retention. Such policies should apply equally to both mothers and fathers and fulfil legal requirements. Many parents want flexibility and reduced working hours so they can spend more time with their families. This can take the form of parental leave (maternity and paternity) and career breaks. In addition to flexible working practices, some employers provide workplace child-care/nurseries or child-care allowances. They may also allow child-care leave during school holidays, organise holiday playschemes, as well as before- and after-school clubs. Provision and requirements should be assessed and re-evaluated regularly as the need for child-care can vary and will be influenced by the size of the organisation, location, existing facilities and financial resources. Questionnaires, covering the number of staff with children, the ages of children, current arrangements and costs, satisfaction with current arrangements, preferred form of child-care, staff planning a family, provide useful information.

Women

Women are a significant part of the workforce but can face a number of issues, such as discrimination, family and domestic responsibilities, lack of career development and being prevented from reaching senior positions. They may leave employment because of discrimination. Pregnancy and childbirth can be seen as contributing to staff turnover and a loss of skills, but career breaks and other creative measures can improve staff retention. Organisations need to consider what will keep and what can help women back into the workforce. If they have been involved in child rearing, they may be more focused on career advancement and professional development in later years. Some issues are the same for any member of staff but what can organisations do to retain women?

- Flexible response to needs
- Flexible working arrangements – part-time, job-sharing at all levels, termtime working, night-time contracts, home-working or a combination of some home-working and time on employer's premises

- Negotiated working hours and contracts allowing women to choose/work those hours that are convenient to them
- Help with child care – workplace nurseries, vouchers, play schemes and opportunities for family leave
- Networking and self-help groups
- Additional maternity pay and extended maternity leave
- Training, retraining, promotion, career development opportunities and career breaks
- Temporary working/self-employment for those women who do not wish to work permanently for an organisation
- Critically evaluate and improve equal opportunities and managing diversity policies to ensure they are not discriminatory. Examine reasons for leaving from exit interviews/questionnaires for evidence of discrimination or gender-specific problems.

Men

Many flexible working practices, including home-working, part-time and termtime working, are attractive to men especially if they are parents. Not all women want to give up work or change their hours especially if they earn more than their partner/father of the child. Opportunities should be available to both men and women.

Young people/school leavers

Younger workers often do not stay in jobs for very long. They have short-term needs and expectations so if you want to keep them you need to put strategies in place to encourage them to stay. Give them feedback, ask for their opinions, listen and be willing to help. Allow them some space and independence but outline clear expectations and goals. Try to keep them interested and reduce their paperwork and administrative duties. Young people (and many other staff) don't like this. Examine rewards and incentives as most young people want short-, not long-term, rewards and career advancement. Job security is not so important.

Graduates

There are shortages of graduates in some subject areas and countries but also increasing numbers of graduates and lack of graduate level jobs. Some find they are given boring and mundane jobs so employers should examine whether they need graduates and be realistic and honest when recruiting. Dissatisfaction and turnover results from development, career and work expectations not being met. Many graduates have high aspirations, want a career not a job, so good quality training and development and career management are important. They will change employers to broaden their experience. Work life balance, working compressed hours to increase leisure time and the flexibility to work from home are also significant. Many graduates expect their effort to be matched by rewards. They have different attitudes, fewer commitments and are prepared to take risks. They need to know they can make a difference, value open communication and responsibility as this demonstrates trust and provides an opportunity to prove what they can do.

Older workers
Older staff often have different expectations, values and work ethic. Be sure you know what their needs are and what you can offer especially if they are looking for job security. Flexible and part-time working are sometimes attractive to mature staff, especially if they have retired early from other organisations. Pay and benefits should also be examined as there are possible pension and retirement implications. Personal development plans and career development (not always vertical) can be important and remember older workers still require training and updating. New challenges, project management and mentoring or coaching roles can be beneficial for staff and organisations.

Senior managers/professionals
As a group, senior managers are often in demand for their skills and experience. They too are viewed as having different needs. Many organisations struggle to attract and keep them and restructuring and downsizing means that many are no longer loyal. Employers need to offer attractive rewards and benefits, training, professional and career development, challenging opportunities, as well as conference attendance, travel, secondments, careers counselling and lateral job moves if they wish to attract and retain them. Transferring or relocating staff, especially overseas, requires particular care. If families are also moving then attention should be paid to arrangements for new home and schools and staff should continue to be communicated with to ensure they feel involved. Employers need to recognise that managers and professionals require support, autonomy and usually have a desire to achieve.

Specialist skills areas

These include information technology specialists, high-performing sales representatives, marketing professionals and other groups in demand. More information technology specialists are required, but with a worldwide shortage, demand is increasing. Training is a major issue in IT staff retention. Increasing costs associated with high staff turnover and missed deadlines are causing some employers to recruit overseas as staff are often less costly but solving recruitment problems is only part of the answer. Sales staff look for recognition and rewards.

Low skilled staff

Retention is also an issue for low skilled staff or those with dirty jobs such as cleaners, porters, refuse collectors and kitchen staff. Listen to them; instil a sense of pride in their work and set realistic targets.

Call centre staff

The number of call centres has increased with a reputation for high turnover. Offer jobs with variety and challenge, good pay and conditions, personal development programmes, training, flexible working and quality working environment to improve retention.

Benefits of staff retention

There are many benefits to retaining staff as we have seen in earlier days. In particular staff retention can:

- Reduce costs of recruitment, selection and training of new staff and makes it easier to recruit new staff
- Keep skills and knowledge in the organisation, particularly important if there are skills shortages

- Improve performance, productivity and profitability
- Improve customer loyalty and satisfaction, can increase sales and aid competitiveness
- Be less costly than replacing staff.

Disadvantages of staff retention and advantages of staff turnover

Employers need to accept that staff will leave and some staff turnover is unavoidable. This can be healthy for an organisation because new staff can bring new skills and ideas. Retaining staff and low staff turnover can cause career blockages, lack of promotion opportunities, an older workforce and lack of new ideas, skills and approaches. It is sometimes easier to introduce change when there is staff turnover. Staff turnover provides opportunities to redesign jobs and change jobs and working practices, such as replacing full-time job with part-timers. Losing staff can reduce some costs by reducing hours and/or recruiting less costly staff or staff employed on lower pay scales. It also provides the opportunity to lose the staff that you do not want.

Costs of staff turnover

Employers need to ask how much staff turnover is costing, as there are costs associated with staff leaving, temporary replacements, recruitment and selection and induction/training. Direct costs are visible and include advertising costs, time for interviewing and administrative costs. Indirect costs are more difficult or impossible to measure such as loss of productivity, financial losses, lost business, low morale and disruption to customer/client services. There are also hidden costs including increased absenteeism, accidents and those who mentally leave by doing the minimum, not volunteering or contributing. There are costs associated with the following:

- Leaving – including administrative time, pay, pension, holiday pay, bonuses, time writing references, exit interviews and questionnaires
- Recruitment and selection – preparing and placing advertisements, correspondence, stationery, postage, administrative time, use of advertising and recruitment agencies, preparing and sending out application packs, shortlisting, staff time interviewing, assessment centres, psychometric testing, documentation for new starters, candidates travel/hotel expenses, medical checks, reference checks, processing of personnel records, payroll, possible relocation or temporary accommodation. These costs can be 150% of the salary of the vacant position
- Induction and training of new staff, involving staff time (trainers/instructors, managers, colleagues, administrative staff making arrangements), equipment, materials and wastage. There may be additional expenses for formal training courses, travel and uniform/protective clothing
- Lost production, poor performance, lack of continuity, reduced service/quality, potential loss of contracts, increase in customer complaints and reduced profits
- Poor initial performance from new/temporary staff. Time needed to develop skills and increase performance
- Loss of skills, experience and knowledge, sometimes to competitors can be costly if key staff
- Increased workload created by new staff and staff leaving, which creates pressure for remaining staff, causing poor morale, lower performance, demotivation and potentially adding further to staff turnover

- Overtime, although if staff shortages no-one may be available to work extra hours and this can affect productivity
- Temporary staff – use of agencies, administrative time arranging extra cover, payroll, recruitment and induction
- Possible risk of accidents resulting from inexperienced staff and/or staff under pressure
- Management time needed for recruitment, training and supervision of new staff
- Lost return on investment if initial training is very long.

Employers should try to measure or estimate these costs and the total recruitment bill as they provide some indication of replacement costs. If an organisation employs 20 staff, has 100% staff turnover per year and the cost of replacing one member of staff is £500, then its replacement costs are £10,000 per year. It makes sense for employers to reduce staff turnover and associated costs but requires time and effort. You should try inserting figures into the following:

> **Your organisation**
>
> Number of staff...
> Number of staff leaving per year.....................................
> Annual staff turnover as a percentage ....%
> Total turnover/replacement cost per member of staff
>   based on costs of recruitment and selection,
>   administration, training, lost sales and productivity,
>   staff time etc...
> Total annual cost..
> Savings if staff turnover reduced by X%
>   (insert your own figure)..

Costs of staff retention

Retaining the staff you want has a direct impact on an organisation's effectiveness and profitability. Focusing on retention can save time and money and improve profitability but you need to know what the costs are, what reductions in staff turnover and costs you want to achieve, and then relate this to retention strategies. Significant costs can be incurred as a result of staff turnover in terms of recruitment and selection, whereas staff retention, as we saw earlier this week, does not always have to be expensive and rewards to staff can be non-financial. Giving someone a day off because they have been working very hard or produced some excellent work demonstrates that they are valued – and costs very little. Similarly, writing a short piece for a staff newsletter recognising the achievement of a team or an individual can be very encouraging. Even rewards that do cost money, such as dinner for two or a small gift, may be a very valuable investment if staff remain with the organisation.

Employers need to critically examine the costs of losing staff and how this affects the organisation and its profits versus the investment needed to keep them. There are strong links between staff retention and business success and failing to do anything about staff retention can have major implications. Actions such as those outlined in Wednesday and Thursday can assist competitive advantage and staff retention, and can be viewed as an investment rather than a cost. High staff turnover can result in the best staff leaving and the weaker staff staying, causing poor organisational performance and a downward spiral, making it even more difficult to recruit and retain staff. Ultimately, this can result in a loss of competitive advantage and damage to an organisation's reputation and may eventually lead to its closure.

Summary

Today, we learnt something about the needs of specific groups of staff, the benefits and disadvantages of staff retention and some of the costs associated with staff turnover and retention:

- Ensure that you understand the needs of specific groups of staff so that you can keep them
- Staff retention can reduce costs and improve an organisation's productivity, performance and profitability
- Some staff turnover is inevitable and it can create opportunities for internal promotion and new staff, bringing new ideas and approaches
- Staff turnover can be costly and includes both direct and indirect costs. You should know what replacement costs are within your organisation
- There are some costs associated with staff retention but view it as an investment rather than an expense. Failing to do anything about staff retention could be very costly indeed.

Who needs to be involved?

Today we will examine:

- Who needs to be involved?
- Summary
- Action plan

Who needs to be involved?

In many organisations no individual or department has specific responsibility for staff retention unlike recruitment, training and development and other people-related issues. As retention is important, organisations cannot afford to ignore it so who should have responsibility for staff retention? It should be shared and involve a variety of people working together and accepting joint responsibility for staff retention. These people include:

- Senior managers/directors
- Managers/team leaders
- Human resource specialists
- Individual members of staff
- Consultants/other experts

Senior managers/directors
Senior managers, chief executive officers and managing directors all need to support retention management otherwise it will not succeed. They need to be receptive and open to new ideas, support recommendations and courses of action, as well as proposing ideas and strategies. They need to demonstrate commitment and integrity.

Human capital and knowledge management are crucial to business success and therefore retention and talent should be senior manager/board level responsibilities and not just human resource specialists. Senior managers and directors should support and develop their own managers as well as measuring their performance in relation to staff management.

Managers/team leaders
They have a very important role in staff retention and need to understand the causes and costs of staff turnover and implement solutions. They can do lots of different things to encourage staff to stay and to improve staff retention. Managers and team leaders need to:

- Recognise that they may be the cause of staff leaving
- Be fair, equitable and consistent
- Receive training and development regarding management of their staff and staff retention – skills in mentoring, facilitation, coaching, counselling, recruitment and selection, interviewing techniques for appraisal, training and development, feedback, dealing with grievances, leadership
- Know that their own performance and effectiveness can be

assessed by staff turnover, staff retention, absenteeism, the achievement of targets and organisational objectives
- Design and define jobs and sometimes redesign jobs
- Be involved in recruitment and selection of staff and ensure job matches abilities and expectations
- Provide induction, initial training and other forms of training and development; recognise potential and assist in career progression and growth
- Recognise that staff are individuals and are different. Understand and motivate them, be aware of morale and job satisfaction and create a positive work climate
- Communicate effectively mission, vision, organisation plans, changes and what is expected
- Be patient, listen and respond to staff, consult and involve in decision-making
- Provide praise, feedback, guidance and recognition on performance and behaviour
- Monitor, measure and evaluate performance using appraisal and other methods; provide coaching, mentoring and counselling to develop staff and improve performance
- Offer constructive criticism and support
- Reward individuals and teams
- Resolve conflicts, protect/defend staff when and where necessary; put procedures in place to deal with conflict
- Be accessible, care about staff, demonstrate interest, deal with personal and professional issues and be sensitive to individual needs. Be courteous, honest and respect staff; loyalty is a two-way process
- Recognise symptoms of stress and take action particularly if individuals are working too many hours. Be a positive role model regarding work life balance
- Demonstrate leadership as this creates trust, a sense of

belonging and should enhance and empower rather than constrain. Leaders are important in creating places where people want to work

- Show real interest in an individuals career both in formal and informal situations
- Share responsibility with staff for their development. Staff should be encouraged to share knowledge and expertise
- Be assessed on their ability to conduct appraisals/performance interviews, discuss performance issues and career development. Their own performance should be measured by their managing director/chief executive officer. This demonstrates commitment and sends the right organisational messages
- Value all staff regardless of their position; provide recognition of contributions
- Provide challenging work, define responsibilities and goals, agree achievable targets and realistic timescales
- Encourage creativity, initiative, innovation, get people involved. Try out new ideas, listen to ideas and help individuals and others develop them
- Select and build teams, facilitate team meetings
- Support staff when they make mistakes and help them to learn. Encourage them to take risks and support them even if they do not succeed
- Treat staff how they as managers and team leaders would like to be treated and work in partnership with staff
- Encourage responsibility and autonomy by effective delegation. Recognise individual freedom
- Recognise and deal with problems such as poor performance and time wasting. If necessary, remove poor staff (including poor managers) as this can have a bad effect on good staff.

Human resource specialists

Some retention specialists do now exist highlighting that staff retention is seen as a major priority for many human resources professionals. Human resource specialists should:

- Be proactive and be aware of issues by talking and listening to all staff
- Work closely with both managers and their staff to ensure staff retention
- Link the needs of staff and the organisation and ensure human resource plans, policies and strategy support each other
- Analyse and survey what is happening within the organisation, conduct exit interviews, monitor staff turnover and follow up after staff have left
- Manage recruitment and career development, review learning, training and development effectiveness and develop managers and team leaders to manage effectively
- Be creative and flexible in the benefits offered, communicate effectively and regularly
- Learn from other firms who have a good record of retaining staff and adjust and introduce new policies.

Individual members of staff

Individuals have a responsibility to be honest during the selection process otherwise their appointment may be flawed. They should discuss their needs and expectations with their manager or team leader. They should also be prepared to act as a buddy/mentor for new staff and possibly coach and develop other staff.

Consultants/other experts
They may be required to conduct exit interviews and
phonecalls, undertake attitude surveys, analyse results
and/or conduct focus groups. They may also be required to
provide specialist advice.

Summary

Staff retention is all about keeping those members of staff
that you want to keep in the organisation. In order to do this
you need to understand what individuals want and also how
organisations and work are changing. Analysis, assessment
and measurement will help you understand this and enable
you to put in place retention strategies that will satisfy both
staff and organisations. No single strategy will work and
whatever strategy or strategies you put in place will need to
be regularly reviewed to ensure that their objectives are
being met. There are costs associated with both staff turnover
and staff retention and you should understand what these
are – failing to do anything about staff retention can be very
costly indeed. However, you should not be alone in trying to
deal with staff retention. A variety of people should be
working together and accepting joint responsibility for staff
retention. Look again at the subjects listed in the introduction
and the summaries at the end of each day to remind yourself
of the main issues in staff retention.

Traditional views of staff retention are no longer appropriate.
It is neither sensible nor possible to offer long term
employment for all and long service does not equal
commitment and loyalty. It is not appropriate to retain all
staff and it is the quality not the quantity of staff that are
retained that is important. Organisations need to accept that

staff will leave and staff turnover is not always negative. Rather than recruit and retain, the emphasis should be on attract, recruit, induct, develop, reward, retain and then separate. Separating positively can result in staff being positive about the organisation.

Action plan

So now we need to put into practice some of the things we have learnt. It is important that organisations recognise the problems caused by staff turnover and set specific objectives to improve staff retention. Organisations need to develop a plan for continually assessing and analysing causes of staff turnover and then take action to retain staff. This is dependent upon two things – that organisations want to reduce staff turnover, increase stability and retention and that organisations know how much it costs to keep recruiting and training staff. Taking action will help improve the situation. You need to **PAUSE** as we saw in Monday. Identify, analyse and understand the problem and why staff retention is important, then set specific, achievable and realistic objectives for a given time period. Remember to evaluate and review how successful you have been.

There are no quick fix solutions to staff retention but the problem can be resolved. It requires effort, hard work, commitment, planning, awareness, analysis and a variety of policies. Keeping staff is a challenge. This book may not provide all the answers but will give you certain options and directions – however the final choice is yours.